RITA D. ZAPATA

KETO DIET FOR BEGINNERS

A Step-by-Step Guide to a Healthy and Sustainable Low-Carb Lifestyle

First published by Rita D. Zapata 2023

Copyright © 2023 by Rita D. Zapata

All rights reserved. No part of this publication may be reproduced, stored or transmitted in any form or by any means, electronic, mechanical, photocopying, recording, scanning, or otherwise without written permission from the publisher. It is illegal to copy this book, post it to a website, or distribute it by any other means without permission.

Rita D. Zapata asserts the moral right to be identified as the author of this work.

First edition

This book was professionally typeset on Reedsy. Find out more at reedsy.com

Contents

Introduction	1
Chapter 1 What is the ketogenic diet	5
The Science Behind the Keto Diet	6
The Benefits of a Keto Diet	7
Who Should NOT Follow the Keto Diet	8
Chapter 2 Getting Started with the Keto Diet	10
Understanding Macros	11
Planning and preparing meals	12
Essential Kitchen Tools and Pantry Must-Haves	14
Tips To Success	15
Chapter 3 Keto Diet Food List	17
Proteins	18
Fats	19
Carbohydrates	20
Beverages and Condiments	21
Chapter 4: Recipes and Meal Ideas	23
Breakfast Options	24
Options for Lunch and Dinner	25
Snacks and Desserts	26
Keto-Friendly Alternatives for Popular Foods	28
Chapter 5: Navigating Social Situations and Eating Out	30
Overcoming Common Challenges and Struggles	31
Staying on Track with the Keto Diet	33

Chapter 6: Maintaining a Healthy and Sustainable Keto...   35
- Importance of Hydration and Sleep   36
- Incorporating Exercise into Your Keto Lifestyle   37
- Managing Stress and Emotional Eating   39
- Monitoring Progress and Adjusting Your Diet as Needed.   40

Chapter 7: Keto Diet Supplements   43
- Thorough Description Of Supplements   44
- Having Trouble Sleeping   46
- Extra Suggestions To Improve Sleep   47
- Recap Of Important Points   47
- Personal Success Story   49
- Conclusion   50

Introduction

The ketogenic diet

You're traveling down a less-traveled path and leading a life that is not for the weak of heart.
However, you are powerful, focused, and ready to make a change. You are also determined.

Eat your fat, don't look back, and leave the carbohydrates in the past.
Your mind will unwind, your body will thank you, and you'll feel better than ever.

Therefore, persevere and don't give up; the ketogenic diet is the best option.
I can assure you that you will be delighted you did.
So just stay on the keto diet.

Millions of individuals all over the world suffer from the terrible health effects of being overweight or obese. Numerous chronic health issues, including heart disease, stroke, type 2 diabetes, and several types of cancer, can be brought on by it.

Although there are many various ways to reduce weight, the ketogenic diet is one of the best. A low-carb, high-fat diet called the ketogenic diet has been proven to be particularly successful in losing weight.

I'm John, and I used the keto diet to shed 100 pounds.

I've always been obese. Nothing appeared to work despite my attempts at every diet known to man. I began to feel like there was no hope.

I first learned about the keto diet one day. I was initially dubious, but I decided to give it a shot.

To my astonishment, the ketogenic diet was effective! My weight loss began fast and without difficulty. I was successful in keeping the weight off, and I soon experienced my best health in years.

My Success Story:

I weighed 350 pounds and was 35 years old. I had become weary of my weight. I was sick of being self-conscious. I was sick of being constrained by my size.

Nothing appeared to work despite my attempts at every diet known to man. I'd lose a few pounds, but I'd quickly put them back on. I began to feel like there was no hope.

INTRODUCTION

I first learned about the keto diet one day. I was initially dubious. All the trendy diets that came and went were things I had heard about. However, something about the ketogenic diet looked unique.

I decided to try it. I began by reading as much information as I could about the keto diet. I discovered that the keto diet causes your body to burn fat for energy instead of carbohydrates. It is a low-carb, high-fat diet.

I was curious. I decided to try it.

On January 1st, 2022, I began the ketogenic diet. I was initially both anxious and excited. I was prepared to change.

The keto diet was difficult over the first several days. I was constantly peckish. I felt weary. I was agitated. But I persevered.

A few days later, the hunger began to lessen. I began to feel more energized. I felt better and better.

After a few weeks, I started to see improvements. I was shedding pounds. I felt much better. I felt more assured.

I shed 100 pounds following the ketogenic diet for six months. I weighed just 250 pounds. I had lost weight. I wasn't sick. I was content.

My life was altered by the keto diet. It aided in my weight loss, health improvement, and confidence-building. I recommend giving the keto diet a try if you are having trouble losing weight. It might end up being the best choice you ever make.

Benefits of Losing Weight

Losing weight has numerous advantages, including:

Improved blood pressure and cholesterol levels, Lower risk of developing chronic conditions like heart disease, stroke, type 2 diabetes, and some types of cancer * More energy * Better sleep quality * Higher self-esteem and confidence

Losing weight can significantly improve your health and well-being if you are overweight or obese. The keto diet can help you lose weight while being safe and effective, and it can also enhance your general health.

Chapter 1 What is the ketogenic diet

The high-fat, moderate-protein, low-carbohydrate ketogenic diet, also referred to as the "keto diet," attempts to support weight loss and better health. The goal of the diet is to put the body into a state of ketosis, where fat is used as fuel instead of carbohydrates. This is accomplished by increasing the consumption of healthy fats and moderate amounts of protein while keeping daily carbohydrate intake at a very low level—typically less than 50 grams. By switching the body's principal energy source from glucose, which comes from carbohydrates to ketones, which come from fat, the keto diet aims to improve blood sugar control, weight management, and other potential health benefits. It's important to know that the keto diet should only be followed under the guidance of a healthcare provider, especially for people with underlying medical issues.

The Science Behind the Keto Diet

The idea of metabolic changes that take place while the body is in a state of ketosis serves as the foundation for the science behind the ketogenic diet. The body typically uses glucose, which is generated from carbs, as its primary energy source. On the other hand, the body is compelled to discover alternate sources of energy when the consumption of carbs is restricted, as in the ketogenic diet.

In this condition, the liver begins to make ketones from the breakdown of fatty acids, which the body and brain can use as an energy source. The name "ketogenic diet" refers to the practice of using ketones as an energy source rather than glucose, which is also the basis for the diet's success in terms of weight loss and improved health indicators.

When the body is in a state of ketosis, it may utilize its fat reserves for energy more effectively, which can cause rapid weight loss, especially in the abdomen. The ketogenic diet may also aid in enhancing insulin sensitivity, which may result in improved blood sugar regulation and a potential decline in the risk of type 2 diabetes. According to several studies, the ketogenic diet may also enhance cholesterol levels and reduce inflammation, among other health indicators.

It's vital to know that, despite the ketogenic diet's potential efficacy, not everyone should follow it, and it might not be long-term maintainable. It can also be difficult to maintain a ketogenic diet when eating out or traveling because it needs careful adherence to the macronutrient ratios. These factors make it important to consult a medical expert before beginning a ketogenic diet and to routinely check one's health markers while on the diet.

The Benefits of a Keto Diet

The advantages of a ketogenic diet could consist of:

- Weight loss: Because the body burns fat instead of carbohydrates for energy, the ketogenic diet can cause quick weight loss, especially in the abdomen area.
- Greater insulin sensitivity: The keto diet may help people have greater insulin sensitivity, which may help them have better blood sugar regulation and possibly have a lower chance of developing type 2 diabetes.
- Increased energy: Many people following the ketogenic diet report feeling more energized and having better mental clarity as a result of switching to fat as their main energy source.
- Improved cholesterol levels: Studies have indicated that the keto diet can raise HDL (the "good" cholesterol), lower triglycerides, and improve total cholesterol.
- The ketogenic diet has been researched for its possible therapeutic advantages in treating several medical diseases, including epilepsy, Parkinson's disease, and specific types of cancer.

The advantages of the ketogenic diet may differ from person to person, and additional research is necessary to properly comprehend its results. It can also be difficult to maintain a ketogenic diet when eating out or traveling because it needs careful adherence to the macronutrient ratios. These factors make it important to consult a medical expert before beginning a ketogenic diet and to routinely check one's health markers while on the diet.

Who Should NOT Follow the Keto Diet

Without a doctor's supervision, the following populations shouldn't adhere to the ketogenic diet:

Women who are pregnant or nursing: The ketogenic diet may not supply enough nutrition for an unborn child or a developing fetus and may even be detrimental to them.

People who have liver or pancreas disease: The liver produces ketones, and defective liver function may cause hazardous compounds to build up over time.

People who have a history of disordered eating: The rigorous macronutrient ratios and focus on weight loss may in some people lead to disordered eating.

People who have kidney disease: The ketogenic diet's high protein recommendations may place additional stress on kidneys that are already compromised.

People who are taking specific medications: The ketogenic diet should only be followed under the guidance of a healthcare provider because it may interact with some medications, such as blood sugar-lowering medications.

It's vital to keep in mind that the ketogenic diet may not be appropriate for everyone, so speaking with a healthcare provider before beginning the diet is important.

Chapter 2 Getting Started with the Keto Diet

Starting the ketogenic diet entails making some significant dietary adjustments as well as having a solid grasp of the macronutrient ratios that make up the diet. To get you started, follow these steps:

Consult a medical expert: It's important to discuss the ketogenic diet with a medical expert before starting it to make sure that it is secure and suitable for you.

The ketogenic diet calls for ingesting large amounts of fat, moderate amounts of protein, and very little in the way of carbohydrates. Calculate your macronutrient ratios. The ketogenic diet typically consists of 70–75 percent fat, 20–25 percent protein, and 10–15 percent carbs.

Create a menu plan: Consider your daily calorie requirements and macronutrient ratios when making your meal and snack plans. Stock up on keto-friendly ingredients for your kitchen, such as lean meats, poultry, fish, eggs, low-carb vegetables, and small amounts of dairy products.

Track your progress: Keep track of your dietary intake, macronutrient ratios, and advancement toward your objectives using a food diary or an app. This might assist you in staying on track and making any required dietary changes.

Gradually transition: It can be difficult to move to the ketogenic diet all at once, so it's important to do so. Start by eating fewer carbohydrates while consuming more fat and protein, then make adjustments as necessary.

It's important to know that the ketogenic diet should only be followed under the guidance of a medical professional and that regular health marker monitoring is required to assure safety and efficacy. It's also important to keep in mind that the diet might not be long-term sustainable and that you should discover a healthy and balanced eating schedule that works for you.

Understanding Macros

The abbreviation "macros" stands for macronutrients, which are the three major food groups—carbohydrates, proteins, and fats—that the body uses as fuel. Following a balanced and healthy diet, especially the ketogenic diet, requires understanding macronutrients.

The body uses carbohydrates, which are present in foods like bread, pasta, grains, fruits, and vegetables, as its main energy source. The nutrition label of a food will list the grams (g) of carbs it contains.

Proteins can be found in meals including meat, chicken, fish, dairy products, and legumes. Proteins are necessary for the body's tissue growth and repair. The nutrition label of a food will indicate the grams (g) of protein it contains.

Fats: Fats are a significant source of energy and help regulate hormones, insulate the body, and cushion the internal organs. Foods like oils, almonds, avocados, and fatty seafood include fats. The nutrition label of a food will indicate the grams (g) of fat it contains.

Understanding the macronutrient ratios that make up the ketogenic diet is important, as is keeping track of your food consumption to make sure you are getting enough of each macronutrient. This can be accomplished by keeping a food journal, utilizing an app, seeing a dietician, or working with a healthcare provider.

Planning and preparing meals

Meal preparation and planning are important parts of the ketogenic diet because they help you acquire the proper macronutrient balance and stay on track with your objectives. The following advice will assist you in organizing and preparing meals:

Make a grocery list based on your macronutrient ratios and food choices, and plan your meals and snacks for the coming week. This can assist you in staying on course and preventing impulsive purchases and bad foods.

Cook at home: Home cooking can save you time and money by letting you choose the ingredients and serving sizes for your meals. Consider cooking in bulk and freezing leftovers for later.

Keep nutritious snacks handy: To help you resist temptation and stay on track, keep healthy snacks like almonds, cheese, and low-carb vegetables handy.

Create original recipes: Try out various cooking methods and recipes to keep your meals interesting and diverse. Look for dishes that incorporate items that are suitable for the keto diet, such as coconut oil, avocado, and almonds.

Use leftovers: To save time and prevent food waste, use leftovers and incorporate them into new dishes.

knowing that everyone has various needs can help you establish a meal plan that suits your needs and satisfies your objectives. Consider consulting a dietician or other nutrition specialist if you feel you may benefit from further direction or support.

Essential Kitchen Tools and Pantry Must-Haves

Certain kitchen gadgets and pantry essentials come in handy when on the ketogenic diet to make meal preparation and cooking quicker and more pleasurable. Here are some pantry essentials and necessary cooking tools:

Kitchen utensils

Cutting board and sharp knife: For chopping vegetables, meats, and other ingredients, you'll need a cutting board and a sharp knife.

Pan: For frying and cooking food, a high-quality skillet and saucepan are required.

Use a blender or food processor to create sauces, smoothies, and other meals that are suitable for the keto diet.

Measuring cups and spoons are necessary for precisely measuring ingredients and guaranteeing that you are consuming the proper ratio of macronutrients.

Scale: Tracking your macronutrient consumption and measuring portions precisely both require the use of a food scale.

pantry essentials:

Stock up on healthy oils to use for baking and cooking, such as coconut oil, olive oil, and avocado oil.

> Nuts and seeds: Nuts and seeds are excellent sources of protein and healthy fats, making them perfect for snacking and incorporating into meals.
>
> Low-carb flours: Have low-carb flours on hand for baking and preparing low-carb baked products. Examples include almond flour and coconut flour.
>
> Sweeteners: Have erythritol, stevia, and monk fruit sweetener on hand to add sweetness to dishes and beverages.
>
> Low-carb vegetables: Have a selection of low-carb vegetables on hand for salads, stir-fries, and other keto-friendly foods. Examples include broccoli, spinach, and kale.

It might be simpler and more pleasurable to follow the ketogenic diet and keep on track with your goals if you have these key kitchen gadgets and pantry must-haves on hand.

Tips To Success

The following advice can help you succeed with the ketogenic diet:

1. Know your macronutrient ratios: Keeping track of your consumption and understanding the macronutrient ratios of the ketogenic diet can help you stay on track and reach your objectives.
2. Plan your meals: Making a plan for your meals and snacks will keep you organized and prevent you from making rash, unhealthy decisions.
3. Cook at home: Home cooking can save you time and money by letting you choose the ingredients and serving sizes for your meals.
4. Keep nutritious snacks on hand: Keeping healthy and keto-friendly snacks on hand can help you resist temptation and stay on track. Examples include almonds, cheese, and low-carb vegetables.
5. Get support: To help you stay motivated and on track, surround yourself with a supportive community, whether it be friends, family, or an online group.
6. Be patient: You may need some time to adjust to the ketogenic diet and you may have short-term negative effects.

Chapter 3 Keto Diet Food List

The ketogenic diet is a low-carb, high-fat eating plan that limits carbohydrate intake while promoting the consumption of beneficial fats. Following is a list of typical foods found on a ketogenic diet:

Meats: Animal products including beef, hog, chicken, and fish are excellent providers of healthful fats and protein.

Low-carb vegetables: Leafy greens like spinach, kale, and lettuce, as well as other low-carb vegetables like bell peppers, broccoli, and cauliflower, are excellent for giving your meals more substance and nutrients.

Nuts and seeds: Nuts and seeds are rich in fiber and good fats. A few examples are almonds, pecans, chia seeds, and flax seeds.

Olive oil, avocado oil, coconut oil, and other healthy oils are excellent for cooking and adding healthy fats to your diet.

Dairy: Dairy products, such as Greek yogurt, cream cheese, and butter, are rich in healthy fats and can enhance the flavor and creaminess of your food.

Low-carb sweeteners: You may sweeten foods and beverages without adding carbs by using keto-friendly sweeteners like erythritol, stevia, and monk fruit sweetener.

There are many other options to pick from, but these are some of the items that are commonly a part of a ketogenic diet. To maintain a healthy and sustained low-carb diet, it's critical to choose foods that are nutrient-dense, high in healthy fats, and low in carbohydrates.

Proteins

Macronutrients like proteins have an important function in the body. They are composed of lengthy chains of amino acids and are vital for a variety of physiological functions, including the development and repair of tissues, the production of hormones and enzymes, and the maintenance of a strong immune system.

Proteins are necessary for human health and should be consumed in sufficient amounts. To make sure that the body receives all of the necessary essential amino acids, it is important to choose high-quality protein sources, such as meat, chicken, fish, dairy, eggs, and legumes.

Protein consumption on a ketogenic diet is typically moderate and should be adequate to support muscle mass and other physiological functions. It's critical to keep an eye on your protein intake and avoid overindulging because too much protein might disturb the ketosis state by being converted to glucose.

To support general health and well-being, it's important to prioritize eating nutrient-dense, whole foods and to minimize processed foods and added sugars. This is in addition to consuming high-quality protein sources.

Fats

Fats are essential macronutrients for the human body. They assist cell growth and development, aid in the absorption and transportation of fat-soluble vitamins, and provide energy. There are several kinds of fats, such as trans, unsaturated, and saturated fats.

When following a ketogenic diet, fat serves as the primary energy source and makes up roughly 70–80% of daily caloric consumption. It is vital to minimize or stay away from dangerous sources of fat, such as trans fats and partially hydrogenated oils, and to choose high-quality, healthy fats, such as olive oil, avocado oil, coconut oil, butter, ghee, and fatty seafood.

The body gains many advantages from healthy fats, such as enhanced heart health, less inflammation, and enhanced cognitive performance. They are important for entering and staying in a state of ketosis as they give the body the energy it requires to function.

It's critical to keep an eye on your fat consumption and avoid going overboard because doing so can result in weight gain and other health problems. To promote general health and well-being, it's important to prioritize eating nutrient-dense, whole foods and to avoid eating too many processed meals and added sweets.

Carbohydrates

Carbohydrates are macronutrients that are present in a wide variety of diets and give the body energy. They can be stored as glycogen in the muscles and liver and are converted into glucose, which the body uses for energy.

A ketogenic diet restricts carbohydrate intake to a very small amount, typically less than 50 grams per day. This limits the body's ability to produce glucose and drives it to turn to use fat as its main energy source, a metabolic state known as ketosis.

Grains, fruits, vegetables, dairy products, sweets, and grains are just a few of the foods that contain carbohydrates. To support the state of ketosis and encourage weight loss, it's critical to choose low-carbohydrate foods like leafy greens, berries, and nuts and to restrict or stay away from high-carbohydrate items like pasta, bread, and sugary beverages.

To promote general health and well-being, it's important to avoid processed foods and added sugars, prioritize eating nutrient-dense, whole foods, and limit carbohydrate intake. To support weight reduction and health goals, it's important to monitor carbohydrate intake and make necessary adjustments to keep the body in a state of ketosis.

Beverages and Condiments

Beverages and condiments play a significant role in the diet and have a big impact on how well a ketogenic diet works.

On a ketogenic diet, it is advised to minimize or avoid alcohol and sugary drinks in favor of water, tea, coffee, and sparkling water. Some sweeteners are thought to be keto-friendly and may be used sparingly, including stevia, erythritol, and monk fruit.

Sauces, dressings, and spreads are examples of condiments that might include a lot of added sugar and carbs. To prevent hidden carbohydrates, it's important to select low-carbohydrate options like olive oil, vinegar, mustard, and mayonnaise and to carefully read labels.

To maintain general health and well-being, it's important to prioritize eating nutrient-dense, whole foods and to minimize processed meals and added sugars in addition to choosing keto-friendly beverages and condiments. To support weight reduction and health goals, it's important to monitor carbohydrate intake and make necessary adjustments to keep the body in a state of ketosis.

Chapter 4: Recipes and Meal Ideas

A ketogenic diet's meal plans and recipes are important components since they help to maintain variety and make the diet fulfilling and pleasurable.

A typical ketogenic meal might have a protein source, like chicken, beef, or fish, as well as healthy fats, like avocado or olive oil, and low-carb veggies, such as broccoli or leafy greens.

Salads, stir-fries, soups, and casseroles are just a few of the mouthwatering and simple ketogenic dishes accessible. Eggs, cheese, nuts, and oils are some common ketogenic items that can be combined to make a variety of delectable dishes.

To support general health and well-being, it's important to prioritize eating nutrient-dense, whole foods and to minimize processed foods and added sweets. This is in addition to adhering to ketogenic meal suggestions and recipes. To support weight reduction and health goals, it's important to monitor carbohydrate intake and make necessary adjustments to keep the body in a state of ketosis.

Breakfast Options

On a ketogenic diet, breakfast is an important meal that can influence the remainder of the day. There are a variety of delicious and healthful breakfast options, such as:

> Eggs: Eggs are a fantastic choice for a quick and filling breakfast and can be scrambled, fried, or boiled. For more flavor and good fats, combine them with bacon, sausage, cheese, or avocado.
>
> Smoothies: Keto-friendly sweeteners like stevia or monk fruit can be used to sweeten low-carb smoothies. They can also be made with almond milk, coconut milk, or heavy cream.
>
> Chia pudding: To make a tasty and filling pudding, blend chia seeds with almond or coconut milk. To add taste and nutrients, this can be sweetened with a keto-friendly sweetener and topped with berries or nuts.
>
> Avocado toast: Slices of avocado can be spread on low-carb bread, like flaxseed or almond flour bread, to make a satisfying and healthy breakfast.
>
> Omelets: A quick and filling breakfast choice is an omelet with vegetables, cheese, and ham or bacon.

CHAPTER 4: RECIPES AND MEAL IDEAS

To enhance general health and well-being, it's important to prioritize eating nutrient-dense, whole foods and to limit processed meals and added sweets. This goes beyond adhering to ketogenic breakfast options. To support weight reduction and health goals, it's important to monitor carbohydrate intake and make necessary adjustments to keep the body in a state of ketosis.

Options for Lunch and Dinner

On a ketogenic diet, lunch and supper alternatives can be delectable, filling, and simple to prepare. Several possibilities are:

> Salads: A salad with leafy greens, like spinach or kale, and a protein source, like chicken, fish, or steak, coupled with healthy fats, like avocado or olive oil, can be a wholesome and full alternative.
>
> Stir-fries: A quick and simple alternative for lunch or dinner can be a stir-fry cooked with a protein source, such as chicken, beef, or shrimp, and low-carb veggies, such as broccoli, cauliflower, or bell peppers.
>
> Soups: A warming and filling alternative for lunch or dinner can be a hearty soup like chicken soup,

vegetable soup, or chili.

Casseroles: A delicious and quick-to-make choice is a casserole cooked with a protein source, such as chicken, beef, or ground turkey, and low-carb vegetables, like zucchini, spinach, or cauliflower.

Meats that have been grilled or roasted: Meats that have been grilled or roasted, like chicken, steak, or fish, can be served with low-carb vegetables, like asparagus, green beans, or Brussels sprouts, to provide a satisfying and healthy lunch or dinner.

To maintain general health and well-being, it's important to prioritize eating nutrient-dense, whole foods and to avoid processed meals and added sugars. This is in addition to adhering to ketogenic lunch and dinner selections. To support weight reduction and health goals, it's important to monitor carbohydrate intake and make necessary adjustments to keep the body in a state of ketosis.

Snacks and Desserts

On a ketogenic diet, snacks and desserts can be tasty and enjoyable while still promoting a low-carb lifestyle. Several

CHAPTER 4: RECIPES AND MEAL IDEAS

possibilities are:

> Almonds, pecans, and macadamia nuts are a few examples of nuts that can make a substantial and wholesome snack.
>
> Cheddar, Swiss, or brie cheese, for example, can be a filling snack option that is rich in good fats.
>
> Berries: Berries, such as strawberries, raspberries, or blackberries, can be a tasty and healthy snack option. However, it's important to watch your portion sizes as berries do include some carbohydrates.
>
> Fat bombs: Fat bombs are little, bite-sized treats that can be sweetened with a keto-friendly sweetener like stevia or monk fruit. They are produced using healthy fats like butter or coconut oil.
>
> Dark chocolate: Dark chocolate, which has a high cacao content, can make for a filling and sweet snack, but it's vital to choose a variety that contains little added sugars.

Desserts that support a ketogenic diet can be created with almond flour, coconut flour, or other low-carbohydrate components, such as keto-friendly cheesecake, brownies, or cookies.

To maintain general health and well-being, it's important to prioritize consuming nutrient-dense, whole foods and to avoid processed meals and added sweets, in addition to adhering to ketogenic snacks and dessert options. To support weight reduction and health goals, it's important to monitor carbohydrate intake and make necessary adjustments to keep the body in a state of ketosis.

Keto-Friendly Alternatives for Popular Foods

Many common items can be converted to the keto diet with a few straightforward changes. Following are some common dishes and their keto-friendly substitutes:

> Bread: Instead of traditional bread, use a keto-friendly alternative like bread made with almond or coconut flour or use lettuce leaves as a wrap.
>
> Pasta: Use spaghetti squash as an alternative to traditional pasta or choose a low-carbohydrate option like zucchini noodles or shirataki noodles.
>
> Rice: Choose a low-carbohydrate substitute for conventional rice, like cauliflower rice or broccoli rice.

Potatoes: Choose turnips, rutabaga, or radishes as a low-carb substitute for traditional potatoes.

Pizza: Instead of ordering traditional pizza, choose a low-carb version with almond flour or cauliflower crust, or add portobello mushroom caps.

Snacks: Choose low-carbohydrate alternatives like celery sticks or kale chips in place of high-carb snacks like crackers or chips.

It is feasible to continue eating popular foods while adhering to a ketogenic diet and leading a low-carb lifestyle by adopting these easy alternatives. To promote general health and well-being, it is important to emphasize eating nutrient-dense, whole foods and limit processed meals and added sugars. To support weight reduction and health goals, it's important to monitor carbohydrate intake and make necessary adjustments to keep the body in a state of ketosis.

Chapter 5: Navigating Social Situations and Eating Out

Following a ketogenic diet can make navigating social situations and eating out difficult, but with some planning and flexibility, it is possible to enjoy meals with friends and family while still staying on track. Some pointers for eating out while following a ketogenic diet in social contexts include:

- In advance: Plan your order by doing some prior research on the menu alternatives. If you have any questions or specific requirements, call the restaurant in advance.
- Express your needs: Inform your server or a host of your dietary limitations and request any suggestions or additional instructions.
- Choose carefully: Choose meals that are low in carbs and high in protein and healthy fats. Try to choose recipes that have fish, vegetables, and meats that have been baked or grilled.
- Adjust as necessary: To suit your preferences, ask for sauce or dressing on the side or ask for a meal to be made without a particular component.

- Bring your own: To make sure you have something to eat if you're going to a potluck or barbecue, think about bringing a dish that complies with your dietary requirements.
- Don't be scared to stand out: It's acceptable to have various dietary restrictions and preferences, and it's important to put your health and well-being first.

Following a ketogenic diet while navigating social situations and eating out is achievable if you use these suggestions and are conscious of your decisions.

Overcoming Common Challenges and Struggles

A ketogenic diet might have its unique hurdles and difficulties. But these obstacles can be surmounted with a little work and grit. The following are some typical difficulties and struggles with the keto diet:

Adaptation period: As the body gets used to a new way of eating, the first few days or weeks of a ketogenic diet can be difficult. Headaches, weariness, and nausea are typical signs throughout this transition phase.

Cravings: It might be challenging to fight the urge to eat meals high in sugar or carbohydrates. To get beyond this obstacle, it's important to prepare meals and snacks in advance and to always have wholesome snacks on hand.

Meal planning and preparation: Making meals from scratch can take a lot of effort, but it's vital to follow the ketogenic diet's dietary requirements. Making sure there are always healthy options accessible and reducing stress can both be achieved through meal planning and preparation.

Social situations: Maintaining a ketogenic diet when dining out or interacting with friends and family might be difficult. Planning, communicating your dietary restrictions, and being aware of your options are important.

Lack of variety: The ketogenic diet can be difficult to vary, especially when it comes to meals and snacks. It's important to experiment with new recipes and ingredients, as well as look for keto-friendly substitutes for conventional high-carbohydrate foods, to overcome this problem.

Cost: Consuming a diet heavy in protein and healthy fats can be more expensive than eating a diet strong in carbohydrates. Planning meals and snacks ahead of time, purchasing in bulk, and keeping an eye out for promotions and discounts on healthy food items are all important strategies for overcoming this difficulty.

It is possible to successfully follow a ketogenic diet and enjoy the advantages of a healthy and sustainable low-carb lifestyle by being aware of these difficulties and having plans in place to overcome them.

CHAPTER 5: NAVIGATING SOCIAL SITUATIONS AND EATING OUT

Staying on Track with the Keto Diet

The keto diet, often known as a low-carb, high-fat diet, can assist you in losing weight and enhancing your general health. The following advice will assist you in sticking to your keto diet:

Plan your meals: Make a list of the things you'll need for each meal in advance to make sure you have them on hand and to help you resist the urge to eat anything that isn't on your diet.

Keep an eye on your macros: The keto diet requires you to keep an eye on your protein, fat, and carbohydrate intake. Make sure you're staying within your macro objectives by tracking your food intake with a meal-tracking app.

Stock up on good fats: The keto diet depends heavily on good fats. To ensure you have a wide selection of healthy fats available, stock up on nuts, seeds, avocados, olive oil, coconut oil, and avocado oil.

Avoid processed foods because they frequently include a lot of carbohydrates and can cause you to enter ketosis. Aim to consume only entire, organic foods, such as meats, veggies, and healthy fats.

Drink lots of water: Hydration is important for overall health, and it can also prevent you from feeling hungry and deviating from your diet.

Find healthy alternatives: Look for a keto-friendly alternative if you're craving anything sweet or starchy. Instead of a typical carb-heavy supper, you might try a low-carb dessert or a dish based on cauliflower.

Be patient; it may take some time to get used to the keto diet and to start seeing its effects. You will eventually reap the rewards of your diligent effort if you persevere and have patience.

You can stay on track with the keto diet and reap all of its advantages by paying attention to these pointers.

Chapter 6: Maintaining a Healthy and Sustainable Keto Lifestyle

Although it takes work and discipline to maintain a healthy and sustained ketogenic lifestyle, the rewards can be significant. Here are some pointers to support your sustainable and healthy keto lifestyle:

Emphasize entire foods: The mainstay of your diet should be whole foods including meat, veggies, and healthy fats. Try to limit processed food intake and prepare straightforward meals.

Listen to your body: Take note of how you feel after consuming certain foods, and adjust as necessary. It can be a hint that you need to adjust your diet if you're feeling run down or having stomach problems.

Maintain hydration: Drinking plenty of water is essential for good health in general and can aid in preventing sensations of hunger that can tempt you to deviate from your diet.

Get enough sleep: Sleep is essential for general health and can aid with diet compliance by lowering cravings and boosting energy.

Regular exercise can help you maintain a healthy weight as well as enhance your general health. Try to get in 30 minutes or more of exercise every day.

Having a support system, whether it be friends, family, or a group of people who share your interests, can help you keep to your diet and lead a healthy lifestyle.

Be adaptable: While maintaining a healthy diet is important, it's equally important to be adaptable and enjoy life. Don't be afraid to enjoy your favorite foods in moderation and give yourself a cheat day every so often.

You may maintain a healthy, sustained ketogenic diet and reap its rewards by adhering to these suggestions. know that this is a journey and not a destination, so be gentle to yourself and acknowledge your accomplishments as you go.

Importance of Hydration and Sleep

Two vital variables that are essential to sustaining general health and fitness are hydration and sleep. Here's why they're important:

Staying hydrated is important for a variety of internal processes, such as controlling body temperature, transferring nutrients, and getting rid of waste. Fatigue, headaches, and a decline in both physical and mental performance can result from dehydration. Getting enough water helps keep you feeling hydrated and energized throughout the day.

Sleep: For both physical and emotional recovery, getting adequate sleep is important. The benefits of sleep include hormone regulation, memory consolidation, and self-healing. Lack of sleep can make you feel tired, make it hard to concentrate, and raise your chance of developing chronic illnesses including obesity, diabetes, and cardiovascular disease. To ensure optimal health, aim for 7-9 hours of sleep each night.

In conclusion, maintaining general health and wellness requires drinking plenty of water and obtaining enough sleep. To ensure that you are working at your optimum, be sure to consume enough water during the day and aim for 7-9 hours of sleep each night.

Incorporating Exercise into Your Keto Lifestyle

Exercise should be a part of your ketogenic lifestyle to maintain general health and fitness and to help you reach your weight loss objectives. Here are some pointers for integrating exercise into a ketogenic diet:

Find a sport you like: Whether it's weightlifting, running, swimming, or hiking, find a sport you like. You'll find it simpler to maintain your exercise schedule as a result.

Establish a timetable: Create a schedule for your workouts and follow it. This will assist you in incorporating exercise into your daily routine.

Start slowly: If you've never exercised before, start at a mild intensity and build up to it over time. This will lessen the chance of damage and make it simpler to maintain your training schedule.

Strength training: Think about including strength training in your schedule in addition to cardio activity. Strength exercise can improve bone density, increase muscle mass, and speed up metabolism.

Track your progress: Use a notebook or an app to keep track of your activities, including your eating habits, exercise routine, and emotional state. You can use this to keep yourself motivated and to gauge your progress.

Be consistent: When it comes to adding exercise to your keto diet, consistency is essential. Make exercise a non-negotiable component of your daily routine by trying to do it at the same time every day.

Get inventive: If you're pressed for time, think about fitting brief exercise sessions into your day. For instance, while watching TV, you could perform some jumping jacks or push-ups.

To maintain general health and fitness and to support weight loss, it's critical to incorporate exercise into your ketogenic lifestyle. To include exercise in your daily schedule, pick an activity you enjoy, create a program, and stick to it.

Managing Stress and Emotional Eating

Maintaining a healthy lifestyle can be extremely challenging while dealing with stress and emotional eating. Here are some pointers for preventing stress eating:

- Become more observant of your thoughts and emotions by engaging in mindfulness practices. This will help you stop emotional eating. To manage stress, try engaging in mindfulness practices like meditation or deep breathing.
- Find good coping strategies: When you're anxious or upset, try to find healthy coping strategies that work for you, such as exercise, reading, or spending time with friends and family.
- Prepare nutritious meals and snacks in advance and keep a variety of healthful foods close at hand. By doing this, you can prevent yourself from grabbing harmful meals when you're anxious or emotional.
- Sleep is essential for controlling stress and lowering cravings. For a restful night's sleep and improved stress management, aim for 7-9 hours each night.
- Control your ideas by attempting to rephrase unfavorable

ones and concentrating on uplifting self-talk. This can help you stay relaxed and upbeat by preventing feelings of stress and anxiety.
- Make friends: Making friends can help you control stress and emotional eating. Connecting with others can make you feel more supported and less alone, whether it be through social support, therapy, or a support group.

Consider obtaining professional assistance if you're having trouble with stress eating or emotional eating. A therapist or counselor can assist you in learning coping mechanisms and resolving any underlying problems that might be causing your stress eating or emotional eating.

In summary, sustaining a healthy and sustainable lifestyle requires controlling stress and emotional eating. To help you stay on track, try mindfulness, healthy coping techniques, planning, getting enough sleep, managing your thoughts, connecting with others, and seeking professional help as necessary.

Monitoring Progress and Adjusting Your Diet as Needed.

Achieving your health and wellness objectives and keeping up a healthy, sustainable ketogenic lifestyle depend on tracking progress and making necessary dietary changes. Here are some pointers for tracking the development and modifying your diet:

Follow your progress: Keep tabs on your development by keeping note of your weight, physical attributes, and emotional state. You can use this to gauge your progress and spot any areas that require improvement.

Keep a food journal to record what you eat and how much you consume to remain careful of your caloric intake. By doing so, you can find out where you could be lacking and make the necessary corrections.

Pay attention to how you feel after consuming various foods. Listen to your body. Consider changing your diet to remove or cut back on certain foods if you have any unfavorable symptoms, such as bloating or exhaustion.

Consider obtaining professional advice from a qualified dietitian or certified nutritionist if you're having trouble keeping up a healthy and sustainable ketogenic lifestyle. They can assist you in coming up with a specific meal plan that suits your requirements and objectives.

Consider trying various diets, such as a higher-protein ketogenic diet or a cyclical ketogenic diet, if you're not getting the results you're looking for. Find what suits you the best, then stay with it.

Don't be too hard on yourself: It takes time to make dietary adjustments, so practice patience and kindness toward yourself. If you make a mistake or don't get results right away, don't be too hard on yourself. You will eventually get the outcomes you want if you continue to make little, long-lasting adjustments.

To sum up, maintaining a healthy and sustainable ketogenic lifestyle and attaining your health and wellness goals need monitoring progress and making necessary dietary adjustments. To make sure you are on the right path to success, monitor your progress, practice mindful eating, pay attention to your body, seek professional advice, try out various diets, and be kind and patient with yourself.

A low-carb, high-fat diet known as the keto diet has been proven to be particularly beneficial for shedding pounds and enhancing health. The keto diet can be difficult to follow, though, and those who follow it frequently encounter several difficulties.

Chapter 7: Keto Diet Supplements

Keto diet supplements are dietary aids that support people in adhering to a ketogenic diet. Electrolytes, magnesium, and fiber are just a few of the necessary components that these supplements can supply that may be lacking in a ketogenic diet. They can also facilitate ketosis more quickly and increase the diet's longevity.

> MCT oil: MCT oil is an easily absorbed kind of fat that has been shown to increase energy and enhance cognitive function.
> Ketone bodies that are created outside of the body are known as exogenous ketones. They can act as a source of brain energy and aid in accelerating the ketosis process.
>
> Fish oil: Omega-3 fatty acids, which are found in fish oil in good amounts, have been linked to several health advantages, including lowering inflammation and enhancing heart health.
> Magnesium: People who follow a ketogenic diet

frequently lack this vital element. Magnesium can aid in enhancing sleep quality, reducing exhaustion, and boosting energy levels.

Vitamin D: An important ingredient for the health of bones is vitamin D. Due to the keto diet's potential to decrease the body's capacity to absorb vitamin D from sunshine, people who follow it may be at risk of vitamin D insufficiency.

Thorough Description Of Supplements

MCT oil is a form of fat that can be discovered in coconut oil and palm oil. Medium-chain triglycerides, or MCTs, are fatty acid chains that are shorter than the lengthy chains seen in most other fats. MCT oil can be utilized as energy because it is readily absorbed by the body. Additionally, it has been demonstrated to enhance cognitive function and enhance physical performance.

Exogenous ketone bodies: Ketone bodies created outside of the body are referred to as exogenous ketones. When the body is in a state of ketosis, the liver begins to create ketones. Your body will begin to spontaneously create ketones once you start a ketogenic diet. To speed up the ketosis process or give the brain a source of energy, exogenous ketones may be beneficial for some people.

CHAPTER 7: KETO DIET SUPPLEMENTS

Fish oil (plural: Omega-3 fatty acids, which the body cannot make on its own and are important fatty acids, can be found in fish oil. Numerous health advantages of omega-3 fatty acids have been demonstrated, including the reduction of inflammation, enhancement of heart health, and prevention of cognitive decline.

Magnesium: Magnesium is a vital mineral that is essential for numerous biological processes, including the production of energy, the health of muscles and nerves, and the regulation of blood sugar. Magnesium deficiency is widespread, and those who follow the ketogenic diet may be more susceptible to it. Supplemental magnesium can aid with energy levels, fatigue reduction, and sleep quality.

Vitamin D: an important ingredient for the health of bones is vitamin D. When skin is exposed to sunshine, vitamin D is created in the body. However, due to the keto diet's potential to diminish the body's capacity to absorb vitamin D from sunshine, persons who follow it may be at risk of vitamin D deficiency. Taking vitamin D pills helps support normal vitamin D blood levels.

It's important to know that dietary supplements shouldn't be utilized in place of a balanced diet and active lifestyle. Consult your doctor before using any keto supplements, if you are thinking about doing so.

Having Trouble Sleeping

When you initially begin the keto diet, it's normal to have difficulties sleeping. This is a result of your body shifting to using fat as fuel rather than carbohydrates. Following the keto diet, you might try these techniques to have better sleep:

* Maintain a regular sleeping routine. Even on weekends, go to bed and get up at the same time every day. This will support the natural sleep-wake cycle of your body.
  * Establish a calming nighttime ritual. This could entail relaxing activities like taking a warm bath, reading or listening to music. Avoid using electronics or watching TV at the hour before bed since the blue light they create can disrupt sleep.

* Ensure that your bedroom is cold, quiet, and dark. Melatonin is a hormone that aids in regulating sleep, and it is produced more readily in the dark. Make your bedroom as dark and silent as you can because noise and light can make it difficult to fall asleep. A chilly environment is also best for sleeping.
  * Avoid drinking alcohol and caffeine before bed: Both alcohol and caffeine might make it difficult to fall asleep. Alcohol can disturb sleep later in the night, while caffeine, a stimulant, might make it difficult to fall asleep.
  * Get regular exercise: Exercise might enhance the quality of sleep. Exercise shouldn't be done too soon before bed, either, as this can make it hard to fall asleep.
  * If you have problems falling asleep Consult your doctor if you have difficulties sleeping for more than two weeks. Your difficulties sleeping could be brought on by a medical ailment

that is underlying.

Extra Suggestions To Improve Sleep

Be sure to consume adequate electrolytes: Minerals called electrolytes to aid in controlling a variety of physiological processes, including sleep. When following a ketogenic diet, you might need to take electrolyte supplements, such as sodium, potassium, and magnesium.

Take a magnesium dietary supplement. A mineral called magnesium is necessary for sleep. It assists in calming the body and mind, which facilitates sleep.

Consider melatonin: A hormone called melatonin aids in controlling sleep. It is available as a supplement that can help with sleep quality.

Consult a sleep expert: You might wish to consult a sleep expert if you have tried all of the aforementioned suggestions and are still having difficulties falling asleep. You can create a treatment plan and determine the underlying reason for your sleep issues with the assistance of a sleep specialist.

Recap Of Important Points

Here is a succinct summary of important ideas to keep in mind when starting the ketogenic diet:

Starting with a plan can help you remain on track and accomplish your objectives. You may do this by making a personalized meal plan and documenting your progress.

Pay attention to your diet: Make sure you are eating a balanced diet that satisfies your individual needs and goals and that you are getting adequate nutrients.

Engage in attentive eating to prevent overeating and make sure you're getting the necessary nutrients for your body.

Keep hydrated: It's important to consume enough water to stay healthy and to keep a healthy weight.

Get adequate sleep: Sleep is essential for stress management, lowering cravings, and feeling your best.

Include exercise: Staying physically active regularly will help you maintain a healthy weight and enhance your general well-being.

Manage your stress and emotional eating by developing good coping strategies and maintaining relationships with others.

Track progress and make necessary adjustments: To make sure you are on the right route to success, monitor your progress and alter your diet as necessary.

You can benefit from a healthy, sustained low-carb lifestyle and meet your wellness objectives by adhering to five important principles.

CHAPTER 7: KETO DIET SUPPLEMENTS

Personal Success Story

Here are a few first-person accounts from successful keto dieters:

> Sarah
> Sarah was consistently obese. She tried every diet imaginable, but nothing worked. When she learned about the keto diet, she had already begun to lose hope. She decided to test it, and she was astonished by the outcomes. She felt better than she had in years after losing almost 100 pounds in a few months.
>
> David
> John was given a type 2 diabetes diagnosis. Despite taking medicine, he still had uncontrolled blood sugar levels. He decided to attempt the keto diet after hearing about it from his doctor. His blood sugar levels were under control and he was able to quit taking medication after just a few weeks on the keto diet.
>
> Jane
> Jane was battling PCOS or polycystic ovarian syndrome. Nothing appeared to work despite the several treatments she had tried. When she learned about the keto diet, she had already begun to lose hope. She decided to test it, and she was astonished by the

> outcomes. She was able to become pregnant and give birth once her PCOS symptoms became better.

These are just a few of the many people who have used the keto diet to good effect. The keto diet might be a smart choice for you if you're looking for a way to reduce weight, enhance your health, or manage a chronic illness.

Conclusion

In conclusion, the ketogenic diet may be a successful strategy for enhancing your wellness. But, especially if you're a newbie, it's critical to approach the diet responsibly and sustainably. You can make sure you are adhering to a low-carb diet that is nutritious, balanced and matches your specific needs and goals by using a step-by-step plan. Tracking your progress, being conscious of what you eat, paying attention to your body, getting professional advice, trying different diets, and being patient and kind to yourself are important first steps. By keeping these pointers in mind, you may position yourself for success and take advantage of all the ketogenic diet's advantages.

Printed in Great Britain
by Amazon